THE ART OF LETTING GO

THE ART OF LETTING GO

A Journey to Minimalism and Freedom

JULES HAWTHORNE

QuantumQuill Press

CONTENTS

1 Introduction   1

2 The Concept of Minimalism   3

3 Letting Go of Material Possessions   6

4 Simplifying Your Digital Life   9

5 Letting Go of Emotional Baggage   12

6 Embracing Minimalist Habits   15

7 Cultivating Inner Peace and Freedom   19

8 Nurturing Relationships in Minimalism   22

Copyright © 2024 by Jules Hawthorne

All rights reserved. No part of this book may be reproduced in any manner whatsoever without written permission except in the case of brief quotations embodied in critical articles and reviews.

First Printing, 2024

CHAPTER 1

Introduction

Finally, a catalyst of events has led me to realize that too much stuff had slowly eroded too much of my mental and financial well-being. This is where I looked around and asked myself "Where did all this stuff come from?" and "How do I get rid of it?"

In the seven years since I graduated from college, I had moved a total of seven times. And during those moves, I always shed a good amount of unnecessary belongings. Yet somehow over the years, new stuff would eventually take the place of the old, and I had never quite succeeded in minimizing. Most of our living arrangements were always small, so we came to the final conclusion that we should just live in clutter because we would eventually be moving to a bigger place. Yet somehow during this time, I had become so bogged down with the process of working and maintaining a household that the clutter became acceptable. The bigger place did not come, and I had finally resigned to the notion that I would just remain constantly overwhelmed.

In the past weeks, I asked myself a series of questions that led me to look around and wonder, "Where did all this stuff come from?" It was a simple question with a not-so-simple answer. At the time, I was living in a two-bedroom apartment with my husband, but the amount of stuff we had crammed into that place would only be appropriate for a five-bedroom house. This was the result of a few years of living in the same place. You see, we viewed this apartment as temporary living in our master plan of life.

CHAPTER 2

The Concept of Minimalism

One can think of minimalism as not just a concept but a way to simplify life's existence. Now to simplify one's existence is a very broad statement, so to argue the validity or meaning of that statement, we must break down the concept into segments. By simplifying one's existence, they are putting themselves in a position to live more carefree, reducing stress and disorders of life. This has been widely argued, but there is an obvious cause and effect. By reducing one's stress and living a more carefree lifestyle, they will lead a healthier life and enjoy a more stable emotional state. A more healthy emotional state can open the doors to increased creativity and intelligence, further enriching one's life experience.

Being able to understand a concept that has been widely interpreted is not an easy thing to do. In terms of design, minimalism is the stripping away of the unnecessary, leaving only the essential elements. When utilizing this concept in creating designs, one must find a way to be simple yet effective. The 20th century art movement and group of American artists known as minimalists is a perfect example of embodying this concept. Throughout their work, they demonstrated precise execution, radical simplification, and industrial fabrication, often with a focus on two-dimensional work. While these are examples and a definition of minimalism, we are utilizing the concept in an entirely different way.

Minimalism is not merely a style. It is an attitude, a way of being. It is a fundamental reaction against noise, visual noise, disorder, vulgarity. Minimalism is the pursuit of the essence of things, not the appearance."

2.1 Benefits of Minimalism

One of the most compelling motivations to declutter is the desire to create a more efficient, organized lifestyle. When there is less stuff to manage, there is less to clean and organize, and that means more time doing things that are important. When your house is in order, it's easier to relax in it. Imagine being able to come home and unwind without having to trip over things or shuffle piles of paper. Unfortunately, many of us have not experienced this sensation in so long, it seems like some unattainable dream. But that feeling is real. It is what happens when the things you own no longer own you. This is a major benefit of the minimalist lifestyle. Many people are motivated to live with less for the promise of more freedom. The more things you own, the more your things own you. They dictate what you do, when and how you do it. This may sound dramatic, but the more you think about it, the more you will realize its subtle truth. Of course, some things that you own are benign and do not affect your life in any adverse way. But much of the stuff we own has some type of hold on us. It could be an old term paper or assignment. You may not realize it, but that thing is occupying valuable space in your mind. It could be a gift that you feel obliged to keep because so and so might come over one day and ask about it. The benefit of owning less is having fewer things to worry about and, in turn, more peace of mind.

2.2 Embracing Simplicity

A simple life does not possess a simple way of living. Life is multi-dimensional and simplicity must be applied to every aspect of life for it to be truly fulfilling. Through embracing simplicity we can clear the clutter that stifles our growth. This attitude will prevent the buildup of future clutter. Clutter is a result of the all too common unconscious approach to life. It is the accumulation of lifestyle decisions made without direction which later require the time and energy to be undone. A conscious and intentional life will only add things to our life which serve a greater purpose. This does not mean there is no longer room for fun and spontaneity. These things are no longer overshadowed by the burden of a hundred other things that need to be done or a hundred more things to be obtained. Fun and spontaneity become more meaningful when there isn't too much on our plate and we have time to fully enjoy them.

Simplicity does not mean turning away from progress and success; it means redefining our ideas of progress and success. It is a conscious choice to live with less in order to experience and appreciate more. It is an intentional direction.

Learning to embrace simplicity in life means foregoing the common and obvious in order to attain the rare and valuable. It is a spirit no longer caught in the clutches of consumerism; free to shake the shackles of comparison, cost, and cultural expectation. Embracing simplicity is a choice to find freedom from the all-consuming desire for more. It is stepping out of the race to find that it has no real finish line. It is challenging the idea that disappointment and dissatisfaction are virtues of character. It is a contented step backward onto the rung of more time and less money. It is a way of life that is free from the modern complexities of the Information Age. More importantly, embracing simplicity is an inward journey, a change of heart, and a reordering of priorities. At the center of the simple life is an awakening to the essence of life.

CHAPTER 3

Letting Go of Material Possessions

The less clutter you have, the less there is to clean and maintain; the less time spent on material possessions, the more time is available to do what truly makes you happy. I compiled all seldom-worn garments and accessories and piled them up. I was quite taken aback by the fact that I had no need for those items, yet I so willingly traded my hard-earned cash to obtain them. It was soon after that I had uncovered the minimalism movement.

When you start to declutter, an overwhelming sense of clarity on what truly adds value to your life will develop. People will find that they experience reduced stress and cleanliness of mind. A layout that will ultimately bring peace to one's psyche. It is important to evaluate the necessity of each possession in your life; take into account how much money was spent on it, how frequently it is used, and how it makes you feel. If something no longer holds significant value in your life, you must ask yourself if it is worth continuing to take up a portion of your living space.

When you let go of material possessions, you're making room for much more meaningful values. Materialism has pushed us to an overload of products, causing us to have a craving for more, no satisfaction, and never truly filling the void. From my experience with ridding myself of all materialism, I can honestly say that I am the happiest I have ever been. I have developed a greater appreciation for all that I own, become more financially stable, and enriched my well-being in becoming a minimalist.

3.1 Decluttering Your Living Space

Before starting to declutter, it is extremely important to set your goals. In Sheree Mares Rule's book "Doing Less and Having More," she suggests making a list of what you definitely want and what you think you might want with material possessions. This will give you a point of reference when going through the decluttering process as to the kind of lifestyle you want to create for yourself. "Doing Less and Having More" is a great resource to read for anyone seeking to simplify life and is serious about change.

Last of all, some people attach a huge sentimental value to items from their past or they are holding on to things "just in case" they might need it one day. Note the excuses you are using to keep items. This will give you an idea of the kind of things you are attached to and help you think about why you are so attached.

Next, clutter may be a sign that you are trying to avoid dealing with emotions. Take a few minutes to sit down and think about what you are feeling as you look at your cluttered room. Are you sad, angry, depressed, or anxious about something? Definitely take notes as study participants who wrote about their emotions regarding clutter were able to throw away more items than those who did not. This is a very important step for you to take. Keep asking yourself about what you are feeling as you go through the process of decluttering. You will learn a lot about yourself.

Research shows that women with cluttered homes full of unfinished projects have higher levels of the stress hormone cortisol. Because women associate how their home looks with their sense of self, it makes it difficult to get rid of anything. Perhaps this sounds familiar?

3.2 Finding Joy in Minimalism

    The high life one gets from chucking stuff is immediate upon realizing that the item is no longer needed, as the thing now transforms into means. Items that are sold or thrown away can be a means to obtain maximum money or satisfaction for minimal time and energy. By ridding the surplus belongings, one will find that time formerly spent managing and safeguarding material goods is now time liberated. This additional free time can now be spent in better ways, without the fear of unearthing old projects. With the means that former material possessions have rendered, one is now free to fully apply the virtues that lead to their release.

    To acquire this conservative way of life that results in supreme happiness and contentedness, one must initially realize the key virtues discovered through minimalism. The next step would be to use those virtues to eradicate materialism, and the remaining few will make sprucing one's dwelling a simple job. When chucking stuff, it is always a good idea to keep in mind the virtues discovered through minimalism. By ingraining the virtues deep into the consciousness, the decision about whether or not to keep an item becomes elementary. If an item does not help you apply or manifest the key virtues, then it is dead weight. Simply cast it away. If an item is something that helps the application of a key virtue and is hard to replace, find a place in the neighborhood to keep it. Then reconsider the item in a while. If the item is not used until the next visit, it is sure to be forgotten and is no longer needed. Store the virtues in an easy place to reflect on for later decisions.

CHAPTER 4

Simplifying Your Digital Life

With the overwhelmingly high number of internet text, images and videos, it is easy to bookmark a ton of things for later reading. However, more often than not people forget about them, and there are a lot of tabs to keep loaded for articles that you 'will definitely read later'. It's good to have a good session of cleaning through all of these and actually read them or just admit that you won't and delete them. A similar process can be applied to your smart devices by removing unused apps and organizing your documents. This is not meant to be a one-time task, but rather these habits should be integrated to your behaviour so that you are consistently managing digital clutter.

Start with your computer, most of our work and entertainment revolves around it so it's good to give it a good clean. Keep your important documents organized in a way that you could find them within seconds. By the end of the day, anything that does not help you with essential tasks should be deleted. If you haven't used it for a long time, you probably don't need it. There are a lot of things that could be deterring you from productivity as well, from desktop wallpapers to unnecessary programs, clearing them can help you stay focused.

Don't forget to apply the "Less, but better" paradigm to your digital life. Simply, get rid of absolutely everything you do not need, leaving only the essentials. Physical clutter in our homes is much easier to see than virtual clutter. Virtual clutter is anything that doesn't serve an important purpose. It could be anything from files on your computer to unnecessary apps on your phone. Giving some love to your digital bits may be a trivial thing, but it occupies virtual space which also affects our mind.

4.1 Managing Digital Clutter

An implementation of the Two Minute Rule with digital clutter is to change Unsubscribe and Delete buttons from "are you sure" to immediate effect, making it easier to instantly get rid of unnecessary email and preventing build up in the future. A more recent instance is the easily accessed archive and delete buttons used by Gmail, reducing the time it takes to manage email and effectively preventing the build up of unnecessary emails.

One of the simplest and most popular systems for managing digital clutter is the Two Minute Rule, where tasks that take less than two minutes to complete are done straight away, preventing clutter from building up from lots of small incomplete tasks. This is an easy habit to develop, as consistency is found to be more effective than initial motivation in sustaining behavioral change.

The key to managing digital clutter is to approach it systematically in manageable chunks of time, and using simple and consistent systems that stop clutter from getting out of hand in the first place. This contrasts with the common approach of "spring cleaning," which can quickly become overwhelming and let digital clutter spiral out of control when large periods of cleaning time can't be found.

4.2 Creating Digital Minimalism Habits

Each digital habit will have a specific cue and may have an obvious reward. To start analyzing these habits, it's useful to record them in a journal whenever you catch yourself doing them. At the end of the day, draw up a simple table with two columns. In the first column, list the approximate times when you were using the computer or smartphone.

In the second column, write down what you were doing, and for each action, try to determine what the cue was that triggered the behavior. For example, if you were browsing randomly through websites, the cue might have simply been feeling bored. If you were checking for a new email, the cue may have been feeling uncertain about whether someone has replied to an email that you've sent. This may take time, but the more cues and rewards that you can identify, the more habits you will be able to dissolve.

The solution is not to try and break the habits directly. This is usually an exercise in futility as the existing neural pathways are too strong. What we can do is systematically reduce the appeal of the cues and the rewards and introduce some friction that nudges the behavior in a better direction.

That transition won't happen overnight. Habits are behaviors that have been wired into our brains through repeated actions. They are strongest when there is a cue, an action, and a reward, and they can be incredibly tough to change. In the context of digital habits, whenever we are feeling bored (cue), we may automatically open up a new tab and browse a social media site (action), giving us a hit of information or entertainment (reward). This process quickly becomes automatic. By loading the behavior with benefits and removing any friction or alternative action (like reading an article or writing something), the habit is likely to become ingrained.

The reason most of us are interested in incorporating digital minimalism into our lives is because it has the potential to significantly improve the quality of our day-to-day existence. The idea of maintaining a lifestyle where the things that are truly important to us can take center stage and have room to flourish is a compelling one. To do this, we need to migrate from a philosophy of technology use that is driven by convenience and entertainment to one that is driven by intention.

CHAPTER 5

Letting Go of Emotional Baggage

The removal of clutter from your life is an essential step to minimalism, but it isn't limited to physical objects. Emotions can accumulate and overwhelm us, taking up mental and spiritual space. The extent of emotional baggage varies from person to person, but it always represents memories of the past and fears of the future. These emotions can block us from mental clarity and freedom. Most emotional baggage comes from unpleasant experiences that we either had inflicted upon us or that we created ourselves. This creates anger, sadness, regret, guilt, and other negative emotions. These can last for a very long time and will continue to affect us. If you have a very emotional reaction to an event or person, it serves as an indicator that there may be a deeper issue to address. Take note of which events trigger strong emotions. These are the key events you will need to focus on in order to release emotional attachment to them.

5.1 Understanding Emotional Attachment

A man who struggles with emotional attachment is foremost struggling with his internal fear of separation from the object. His attachment is the result of craving a particular sense of security that he attributes to the object of attachment. He is attached because he believes it brings him happiness. For example, a man might be attached to a vehicle because it provides a means of transportation. He is attached to the security of knowing he can get from point A to point B. A man might be attached to a girl because he feels that she is an important part of his life and that she brings him happiness. He is attached to the security of knowing she will always be there. This point, in particular, is very important because it brings to light the temporariness of every object of attachment. The man is bound to lose the vehicle through auto theft, mechanical failure, or buying another vehicle to replace it. In each case, the vehicle is gone and with it goes the man's sense of security that was based on the vehicle. The same applies to the girl as she is mortal and is bound to perish in some way. When the vehicle and the girl are no longer available, the man will experience suffering as a result of separation from the object of attachment.

5.2 Practicing Emotional Detachment

Emotional baggage can also be from attachment to happy memories. This may sound contradictory because why wouldn't anyone want to keep happy memories? But it becomes baggage when you are stuck on reliving those memories, thinking that the best part of your life has happened. This prevents you from creating new experiences that are just as good, if not better.

Emotional baggage consists of old hurts and wounds that still burden you. It can be the result of past experiences, unresolved issues with others, and negative feelings that you were not able to express. Emotional baggage prevents you from living in the present. It colors everything you see with the tainted glasses of the past. You take it with you into the future and it hinders your growth. Emotional baggage is heavy, it weighs you down. Coming to terms with what you need to let go can be a task that takes much courage, but it is a necessary step towards living an uncluttered life.

Many people say letting go is one of the hardest things to do, but it is also one of the most beneficial. When you let go, you create space for better things to enter your life. When you refuse to let go, you are not living in the present; rather, your mind is consumed with memories of the past. This can cause you to miss out on new opportunities that come your way. Your mind is so caught up with holding onto the past that there is no space for new possibilities.

CHAPTER 6

Embracing Minimalist Habits

This brings us to "living with intention". Ultimately, the habitual goal of a minimalist is to live a more fulfilling, meaningful life by removing the excess in their lives and opening up the time and space to allow them to do more of what they're passionate about. By living with intention, you're able to do just that. You begin by understanding your true goals and purpose in life and making space for them, so that you're able to give your very best to what is most important to you. You begin to choose your actions based on whether they will help you reach your goals and whether they reflect your values. Over time, you'll cultivate a life that is in alignment with your true self, what makes you happy, and what you want to give to the world.

Those who are new to minimalism will very quickly discover that adopting the lifestyle is a journey of introspection and self-discovery. Mindful consumption is about creating an awareness of how and why you're making your consumer choices. It isn't about restriction, denial or guilt. It's about cherishing what's truly important to you by removing the clutter of consumerism. Mindful consumption will very often lead to making more thoughtful, informed and considerate choices which are in line with your values and beliefs. The central message really is to make purchases with great intention, taking into consideration the long-term effects of the purchase on both the environment and you, and whether it truly adds value to your life. By practicing mindful consumption, you'll begin to develop a greater sense of clarity and purpose in your life because you're no longer filling it with items that provide only fleeting happiness. You'll feel a greater sense of fulfillment and satisfaction because you're nurturing contentment through the ability to appreciate and fully enjoy what you do have, and what is truly important: your health, your relationships, your passions, and your personal growth.

6.1 Mindful Consumption

Mindful consumption is a concept advocating that we should acquire and use possessions with more thought, making a habit of asking whether the item is truly necessary. It is a call to sift through our purchases and differentiate between the things that add value to our lives and those that detract from it. A very large portion of advertising is designed to make us think that we will have more fulfilling lives if we consume and buy more. Ads are everywhere and they are very pervasive; because of this, we are constantly exposed to this idea and it begins to seep into our subconscious. Mindful consumption asks us to be more aware of the role these ads are fulfilling and how we are taking them on board. With regular reinforcement, this habit will become second nature and we will learn to become immune from these types of marketing tactics. This form of immune system from the consumer culture will free us from its grasp and help us to live more fulfilling lives. Mindful consumption is also about making smarter choices with your money so that you do not waste it on things you will regret later. The idea is not to stop spending money altogether but to spend it in a more meaningful way. By applying mindful consumption to each of our purchases, we can draw boundaries to what we actually need, vs. what we can do without. With these boundaries in place, we can prevent emotional spending, where we buy things to make us feel better, on a temporary high and future regret. This can be especially helpful in saving money. Finally, at a personal level, mindful consumption can greatly reduce the amount of clutter and stress in our lives. We can rid ourselves of the many things we have bought but not needed and make a commitment to only bring new things into the house that are necessary and will add value to our lives.

6.2 Living with Intention

A healthy lifestyle is something that is invaluable and, of course, something that consumers try to buy into with a plethora of items from supposed superfoods to brand name athletic wear. With intention, these consumers have very different outcomes. The first is someone looking to bolster their image through associating rhetoric and health with luxury. Buying identity and status is a dangerous game with many unnecessary products. The second would be someone who truly wants to be healthy and better themselves. A focus on intention will make this person sit and think about the goals and tools they're realizing they want to change. Eating healthier and doing so with the intention of manipulating habits by getting rid of artificial food is something that will change a person's looking for a specific outcome. This person will want results, convincing them to buy into a healthy item or service, and will lead to using said service. This is the type of behavior that is worthy of a consumer, and intention is a breakable way to stick to doing what is necessary.

Focusing on quality over quantity is a phrase heard time and time again but is never truly taken into deep consideration. Quality is a great measure of an item's longevity and as long as it is of value and purposeful, being a minimalist should not mean exclusion of quality products. Embracing the idea of quality with intention can form habits of conscious buying and learning about what products will last in the long run. It leads to decisions like investing in a non-disposable item because the intention was to always have it. Efficacy is a launching point into many beneficial behaviors with one of these qualities being a managed healthy lifestyle.

To live with intention is to live with purpose. It is to consider what adds value and what does not. It is a way of filtering out the excess that does not necessarily mean material possessions. Considering intentions behind actions can lead the way to making a conscious effort to change habits. For example, someone's intention in wanting to see the world and experience new cultures will mean that spending money on material items would be less of a priority. This person would be less inclined to clutter living space with items and trinkets when there is an intention of long-term travel. With minimalism, it is about making life-changing tidying up the environment so that it can cater to new changes.

Without intention, it's possible to fall into the traps of consumerism even with minimalist habits. Purpose and meaning are very easy to lose when possessions are still forced into the center. Understanding the deeper reasoning behind embracing minimalism is key to making it a lasting change. Living with intention in all areas brings forth what minimalism truly stands for to each individual.

CHAPTER 7

Cultivating Inner Peace and Freedom

Jealousy is a direct result of comparing ourselves to others and is a barrier to inner peace and contentment. It's impossible to live a unique life that is true to ourselves if we are constantly comparing it to the lives of others. It's time to let go of the comparison and instead direct our energy to living authentically and respectfully to our own personal callings. This requires a sense of self-awareness and assurance. When things do not bring us joy, we should thank them for their use or the lesson they brought us and let them go. This practice should be adopted when viewing the lives and possessions of others. If a particular life or possession does not bring us true contentment, then we should simply acknowledge it and work towards our own personal goals to lead a life that does bring us contentment. By comparing with others, we are allowing our egos to make our decisions, rather than our true selves. The ego is never satisfied, and it will always want to have more and be better than others. Step by step, we need to learn to differentiate our egos from our true selves and make our decisions based on what we know to be truly right for us. Our society is much too concerned with the opinions of others, and as a result, a large quantity of our possessions are not owned for our own pleasure but to impress others. When we free up this mental energy of comparing our lives to others, we will also free up physical energy and space by owning only what is necessary and what truly brings us satisfaction. At this point, we can decide to free ourselves from the burdens of an over-complicated lifestyle and make more room for life's truly joyful experiences.

7.1 Letting Go of Comparison

The key to letting go of comparison lies in recognizing the futility of comparing ourselves with others. Instead, we must learn to measure our value based on personally chosen values and intrinsic qualities. We must unlearn the habit of self-judgment and evaluation based on what we do, what we have, and what others think of us. This means being mindful and choosing to be aware when we are falling back into comparing. When we do notice ourselves comparing, we can remind ourselves that our own or another's worth is not determined by what they have, what they do, or what others think of them. By learning to accept and love ourselves for who we are, working on personal weaknesses, and nurturing our positive qualities, we can cultivate a sense of worth and self-esteem that is untouchable by comparison with others. Recognizing that we are all unique and valuable human beings can help to mitigate the feelings of separateness and superiority/inferiority, bringing about an attitude of equality and compassion towards others.

When we compare our lives with others, we tend to measure our worth by people, possessions, and social status. We create our personal identities based on a comparison with others. We constantly measure our worth, value, and success compared to others. Comparison nourishes feelings of superiority as well as feelings of inferiority. It reinforces views of separateness, of being better or less than others. These feelings of superiority or inferiority contribute to inner conflict, jealousy, and envy. They bring about a fear of not being good enough and of not measuring up. This fear brings about feelings of anxiety, insecurity, and that we are not deserving of happiness and success. It is clear that comparison does nothing to foster inner peace and happiness, and as long as we are doing it, there will always be a prevailing sense of discontent.

7.2 Prioritizing Experiences over Possessions

We have been conditioned to desire possessions even more than we desire happiness. Because of our materialistic culture, we have forsaken memories and experience, the intangible, for material goods that have no true lasting value. Consider the nature of back to school rituals. When children reunite, they do not show their happiness by material gift giving. Instead, they swap stories of the places they have been, the things they did. The value of these interactions is immeasurable, for it is shared experiences that build bonds and bring lasting joy. But what of this future generation, when youth conversation sounds like, "What I really want is the new iPhone." They have already been sold the idea that the key to happiness lies in "having stuff." They will grow to be more disconnected from friends, family, and life in general. All the while they will be burdened with stress in trying to maintain that which they have accumulated. Is this truly the American dream?

Thus cultivating a mentality of gratefulness, I learned to view possessions more skeptically. The greatest lesson was uncovering the extraordinary left behind by "the ordinary." I once house-sat for 2 months, living with only bare essentials. My clothes were stuffed into a makeshift closet, economy furniture, and kitchen utensils were scarce. The most cherished part of the home was a beautiful Japanese garden. This experience shifted my view on what brings happiness.

CHAPTER 8

Nurturing Relationships in Minimalism

The other side of this is letting go of toxic relationships. This is potentially one of the hardest challenges. It is very disheartening to imagine that people close to you may not understand or agree with the lifestyle changes you are making, and ultimately, for some people, it may mean the end of connection with that person. In simple terms, the best way to discover these relationships and determine if they are toxic is to weigh up how you feel during and after time spent with that person. If they are leaving you with negative feelings, then the relationship is not good for you. To lead someone else to understanding is also wasteful if it is beyond your control, and the decision to cut ties would have to be made. This can be done gradually and doesn't have to be a direct confrontation, or it can be done by letting the frequency of connection decrease till it is no longer a part of your life.

This is one of the key points I wanted to make in this essay. It is about nurturing our relationships once the materialism is out of the way. We will find that there will be good and bad effects on our relationships with other people. Some of our relationships would have been based on material activities like going to the movies, shopping or fine dining. When this is no longer the focus in our lives, it is likely we will have to change activities with that person or find new people to connect with. This no longer needs to be seen as a bad thing, as it is positive to experience new things and trying to include this person in the change of activity might bring them towards the lifestyle of minimalism too. On the other hand, there are some relationships which are established on deeper connections with the person and not the activities involved. This person would be someone you can easily talk to, have a laugh with, and share problems with. These are the connections we want to nurture, and it is important to note that nurturing these connections will also help nurture that habitual mindset of who you are.

8.1 Letting Go of Toxic Relationships

In recent years, psychology has uncovered that we are heavily influenced by the people we spend time with. Known as Social Contagion theory, it states that both our mental and physical health are closely tied to the behavior and attitudes of our social groups. Studies show that certain attitudes and behaviors can spread, much like the common cold, from person to person, leading to detrimental effects on health. An example might be hanging around with friends who constantly gossip, leading us ourselves to begin gossiping. This can be particularly dangerous because sometimes the spread is so slow and subtle that we don't notice the change in ourselves. If attitudes and behaviors are spread, it's best to avoid people with negative ones.

One difficult aspect of applying minimalism to life is sorting through relationships and deciding which ones to salvage and which to end. To determine which relationships are toxic, ask yourself the following questions: Is the relationship one-sided? Does the person take, take, and take without giving anything back? Is the person overly critical or negative?

8.2 Fostering Meaningful Connections

When we decide to adopt minimalism, we want to make our life simpler and dedicate our time to only what is most important. An important aspect of life is our relationships with other people. It is important to not isolate yourself if you decide to go through a large-scale declutter, as it can be emotionally tough to let go of items and not having to fill emotional needs you get from relationships with material items. One reason people hoard items is for the emotional connection the items represent. Releasing attachment to material possessions is often easier if one has good social support. Having friends to talk to and invite to do activities maintains healthy emotional needs. So, what do we do about people who are "bad for us"? Step one is putting things about our important relationships in writing. We're likely to give a different amount of benefit of the doubt to every person and every situation, but when someone habitually stresses us out to the extent that it is not worth keeping a relationship, it is time to cut the rope. If we are just on the fence about someone, go from yes to a good trial period. People change, and it is quite possible to transform a mildly toxic relationship into a beneficial one. The time it takes to change a sure toxic into a middle ground is more than it is likely worth, but the decision is not always clear-cut, so it's okay to write a list of pros and cons on that person. Lent suggests that we get rid of anything that is not useful or beautiful. If we are stopping at "beauty," we can find something useful for the back of a photo that somehow never made it to Facebook. We can schedule a friend date, and with technology the way it is, there are more ways to keep in touch than ever. When considering ways to maintain communication, take into account what method will be the best way to express emotion. A phone call is a way to actually talk to someone, but a poor choice for venting about noisy roommates, whereas instant messaging is good for a chat, but if we are just chat logging, it is not much different than being alone. Email is a decent compromise between the two. We would likely find it most fulfilling to replace the maximum communication method from the past that was causing a clutter emotional needs. If you are doing a people project, don't forget to directly or indirectly assess the success levels at which you are doing so.

Milton Keynes UK
Ingram Content Group UK Ltd.
UKHW021933050924
447857UK00007B/147